Passing Comets

Front panel of a cabinet in my shop where
Passing Comets have been recorded through the years.

*When I get famous,
I'm going to have to stop writing on the furniture.*

Don Briddell

Passing Comets
By Don Briddell

Copyright © 2021

Published by:

Overboard Art, Inc.
Don Briddell
8002-A Dollyhyde Rd.
Mount Airy, MD 21771

donbriddell@overboardart.com

ISBN: 978-1-7357041-3-5 (paperback)
ISBN: 978-1-7357041-4-2 (epub)

Illustrations, photos, and drawings by Don Briddell and 416 comets as of this publication

"Whatever GOD is, we are."

Swami Bill

Table of Contents

List of Illustrations

Preface

These short comments began popping up in Ecuador where I was serving in the Peace Corps starting in 1967. Since beginning college, I have always carried a sketch book. That enabled me to scribble down thoughts whenever and wherever encountered. Sketchbooks became journals as I traveled and worked around the world. They accompanied me on my mission to understand what life was all about, its quirks and its laughs . In the Peace Corps I met other like-minded "journal-keepers" such as the poets, novelists and artists, John Brandi, Fred Marchman, and my future wife, Victoria Moller. Writing thoughts and experiences down became a useful tool for us in this endeavor.

Leaving Ecuador after two and half years, Passing Comets illuminated my path as my wife and I with backpacks traveled around the world across South America, to Canada, Europe, North America, Philippines, Japan, China, Malaysia, Sri Lanka, India, South Africa, and eventually back to the USA. But it was in my workshop while carving and painting wildfowl and sculpting humans that most of these comets found me. I say "found me" because none of these comets were thought out productions. They came from God knows where and popped into my mind without warning. Always within arm's reach was my sketchbook/ journal to record their arrival with text and sometimes with a drawing. Life is a fantastic journey when it is allowed to unfold as it intends. By not being selective about what you are willing to experience, you get to see not only the top-side of experience, but its underbelly as well.

Usually these comets had nothing to do with what I was doing at the time but everything to do with what questions I was deeply mulling over in my mind. I began to suspect they were not even my comments, but rather they were comets floating around in the cosmos and for some unknown reason like comets in the night appeared without rhyme or reason. The experience is akin to duck hunting, which I used to do as a kid. I would set out in my boat and cruise to a lonely outpost in the marsh by the water's edge, put out a string of decoys and then sit in a duck blind for most of a day waiting for a duck to mistake my decoys for their compadres. What came along was not my invention. So it was with passing comets. They found me but I had to hold the question, which is analogous to putting out decoys, in order to attract the ducks. To realize this procedure has been a great lesson to me and why hunting embodied a great teaching. Putting out the decoys and formulating a question amount to the same thing. I will have no success in life if I don't "hold the question," that is, put out the decoys. Only then, answers will find me. Fortunately, I made the switch from putting out decoys to putting out questions. I have spent the rest of my life since those youthful days in the duck blind making up for the carnage by carving waterfowl on the order something like a hundred carvings to one duck shot in an attempt to work off as much of the karma as I can before I am bagged by the grim reaper.

As to why the comets are in one chapter or the another, I let intuition make the call. There will be some that appear stupid, or inappropriate, or not up to the mark of being worthy. I have found if a comet is disliked by one person, it may be prized by another. With equal force, up-lifting comets have appeared followed in time by downers; there is no escaping the yin-yang nature of reality and there is a teaching in both. No matter whether the comets are lifting or descending, they ask of me to pause and consider, and on occasion, laugh. Eliminating the pushes and pulls of life is impossible and maybe not even a desirable thing to do. If one should succeed totally in pursuing either the ups or downs, all is lost. It's in how you respond, or not respond, that is the art and science of it all.

Language grows in power when the big and complex issues of life can be reduced to as few words as possible and if possible with elegance. It is then that words can, with the economy of a mathematical notation, "say it all." Becoming wordy is unwanted fat. The cosmos likes simplicity. If not overwhelmed by the noise of day-to-day experience, the mind will voluntarily begin to organize life at its deepest level, giving occasional reports that surface. A record of these reports are the passing comets herein. In this way, comets are closing statements, summations of an internal dialog that I have been having over a long period of time.

The visuals in the book may or may not have anything to do with the text near the image; usually not. To me they are interesting visual passing comets which like the text just appeared, not governed by will or intention.

Note that when you read the word "you" in a passing comet, this is me talking to myself.

I regret having to put multiple comets on a single page. My first attempt at putting this book together was to give each comet a page of its own with an illustration. There are hundreds to choose from in my journal/sketchbooks. That would have made a simple little book into a lengthy 426-page tome although it would have added, I think, merit to each comet.

Comets by other authors are credited where they appear. Enjoy!

Chapter 1
Absolute Basics

Fig. 2 Mother Yvonne while she sat in bliss – Sivananda Ashram,
Rishikesh, Himalayas 1971

1. *The longest of all journeys is the one that ends in your heart.*
    Spoken by Swami Chidananda while visiting the Ashram at Harriman, NY.

    - 18 Aug 1975

2. *When you love, life is taking care of you.*

    2018//2020

3. *Consciousness is the creator .... Love is the savior.*
    Parting Words of Mother Rema Veramani as we left her house for the train.

Fig. 3 Photo of Mother Rema Veramani, Madras, India, an accomplished Shakta 1970

4. *You are what you can't quite remember, but have never forgotten.*

15 November 2014

5. *The image of perfection comes in silence.*

12 Mar 1972

6. *Anything you give cannot be taken from you.*

7. *The hands that make a star, make a soul.*

1970

8. *Through the fabric of the universe penetrates the undulating needle of the will embroidering the designs of life.*

a comet on my 40th birthday - 1 Jun 1984

9. *When you're trying to cover the universe,*
   what good are legs?
   When you trying to make a universe,
   what good are hands?
   When you're trying to imagine a universe,
   what use is a mind?
   And when you're trying to be a universe,
   of what use is the ego?   *Early 1989*

10. *Stop allowing the mind to run the show. Upgrade to your higher angel.*

28th March 2017 @ 4:30 AM

11. *Somewhere along the line, God said, "Let there be the details," then all hell broke loose.*

2019

12. *The void is the womb of Reality.*

20 Jan 2013 - dawn

13. *The hand that made you still holds your hand.*

March 12, 1979

14. *Don't worry about the past, it's over and done with. Don't worry about the future, it never comes. Live in the now.*

1998

15. *God provides the facts of life. Humanity turns it into a drama.*

Saturday, 8 February 2014 then again 22 November 2014

16. *Consciousness doesn't need a universe, but a universe needs a consciousness.*

Oct. 2018

17. *Nothing can't ever happen ..... Only something can happen, and it will!*

8 April 2014

18. *Stars are holes in the veil of maya showing the illuminating radiance of consciousness that envelops and pervades the universe like an egg.*

Solarplex (Sunbeam House) Mt. Airy, MD - 8 March 1981

19. *Truth doesn't have a shadow.*

1984

20. *Life is the product of perfection.*

1980

21. *The material universe has forms too numerous to count.*
     The energetic universe has only one form, the loop, too vast to comprehend.

Field Structure Physics 101 - 28 Jan 2018

22. *Miracles happen, but reality is more dependable!*

since time began

23. *Maya is the net effect.*

25 August 1971

24. *Forget the past. The future is being made as we speak.*

17 July 2018

25. *One thing is for sure …. Nothing is for sure.*

18 January 2014

26. *Lying is exhausting. To hide a lie takes a lie, and another and another…*

6 June 2017

27. *Mathematics can't explain what the mathematician can't explain, and yet the theorists keep hoping it will.*

2020

28. *There is a lot in life we love without having to understand it and yet we keep loving it even if we can't understand it. This is humanity at its finest.*

August 21, 2020

29. *The hardest thing to look at is the sun without and the Self within. Both are blazing orbs of light.*

India 1970/USA 2020

Fig. 4 Moo weaving a net to keep birds out of the inner sanctum of the Ashram temple – 1971

30. *There is no money in heaven. The currency of heaven is love and it is only love that you can take with you.*

18 December 2013 – revised 16 Aug.2020

31. *The way to understand truth* is to recognize falsity.

24 Dec 2018

32. *The difference between DOING and BEING is the difference between actualizing and realizing.*

18 Aug. 2020

33. *The important things we know, we know without knowing how we really got to know them.*

34. *It's not how many minutes are in your hour, it's how many hours are in your minute !*

10/19/2012

35. *Awareness of the ever-present field in which objects exist, is a prerequisite for understanding and experiencing the unity that connects the universe.*

Field Structure physics 101 - Aug 1996

36. *We don't create the truth, it's there and we find it.*

29 Oct. 1970

37. *God has more than one suit of clothes. The world is his wardrobe.*

3/14/2016 Sunbeam

38. *Consciousness can organize the universe in an instant and does so instantaneously ….. You are the prime example.*

Apr. 15, 2014

39. *Something from nothing = magic.*
   Something from everything = reality.

29 November 2013

40. *What you are doing …….. is what you are becoming.*

41. *"No Thing" - the nature of reality; "Nothing" - the nature of illusion!*

8-April 2014

42. *God is not the problem. It's how we package Him that gets tacky.*

30 Jun 1986

43. ***In a crazy world ... you need crazy wisdom.***

Fig. 5 And now for my final trick ...   1968

44. ***Your mind is not in command, though it assumes it is. You are not your mind. The commander of your mind is your soul, and your soul is divine. Honor your soul and your mind will know its master.***

Field Structure metaphysics 101 28 Jan 2018

45. ***Life, and all therein, is a mirror that lets you see yourself.***

29 Oct. 2018

46. ***From nature we can hear in its silence the thrilling call of the wild.***

Jan 19, 2020

47. ***Don't let the pursuit of money leave you with little time to feel the soul of the universe in your life.***

Nov.30, 2019 at 75 years old

48. *Life is short. Fortunately, what we need to know is simple.*

Sept. 2013

49. *To experience the utter valueless-ness of all things and then create wealth is crazy wisdom. To see wisdom in the futile effort and delusion in the necessities are examples of crazy wisdom.*

Field Structure metaphysics 101 1976

50.

Big

Ideas

are

often

small

when

compared

to

the

work

it

takes

to

execute

them

51. *Do I live as a verb or a noun? The path is both.*
As a noun, I am a knot. As a verb, I am the string.

Field Structure metaphysics 101 *2018*

52. *The best way to have an idea … is to make a space for it.*

53. *Without nature, how can there be wisdom?*

54. *Cash & carry gurus charge for their services.*
Beware, truth cannot be purchased at any price.

20 November 2014

55. *Near is fast … Far is slow.*
Space slows time … Time expands space.
America has space … and little time.
India has time … and little space.

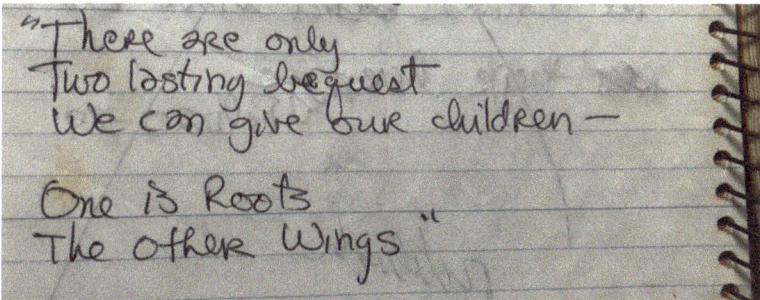

"There are only
Two lasting brequest
we can give our children —

One is Roots
The other Wings"

Fig. 6 Roots and Wings   197

13

56. *Anything can happen, but for sure, something WILL happen.*

2015

57. *If it's dharma ... DIN (do it now). If it's karma ... LIB (let it be).*

April 1, 2015

58. *I'd rather be there ... than talk about it.*

Sept .21, 2015

59. *He who is blessed with a good idea is also cursed with the responsibility of doing something with it.*

Rishikesh, India   8 Jan 1971

60. *In order for anything to remain the same, every-thing must change.* This comet floored me! Is real-ity really that connected? If it is, we are living in awesome.

17 Mar 2014

61. *The problem, as humans see it, is that God has left it all up to us.*

29 Oct. 2018

62.   *We need a faith we can defend without having to kill someone to do it.*

Jun 1972

63.   *The mind can be God's garden or the devils briar patch.*

10 May 1989

64.   *God said to the sage, "What's so funny?"*
The sage paused from his laughter and said,
"I just figured out what you meant!"

Postscript: Startled by this early learner, God said, "Game's over!" and the sage died of laughter.   3/11/2010

65.   *The gift of life is not a gift .... There are bills to pay.*

66.   *Consciousness pervades the process.*   Dec. 11, 2017

67.   *PEACE – nature's box of chocolates for the tortured soul.*

March 21, 2011

Chapter 2
Nirdvandvah

Pronounced: Near dvan dvah

Sanskrit meaning: **"freed from the pairs of opposites"**

Fig. 7 Swami Chidananda at an evening satsang with listener 1971-
Rishikesh, Himalaya

68. Zen is plain *Yoga is fancy*

69. *What I like about meditation is that by doing nothing so much is done.*

1 Jan 1972

70. *The extremes are that at one end there are those who have too much to count and at the other end, those with nothing to their name.*
Sages and saints span this entire spectrum. At once they are so wealthy it staggers the imagination and at the same time, they beg for morning tea.

29 November 2014

71. *Nothing can happen until something happens.*

8th April 2014

72. *When asked what church he goes to,*
the pious man said, "I go to 'such and such' church."
The sage said, "All churches are my church."
The Vedantin said, "I am the church."

31 Aug, 2017

73. *In a room full of triangles, in walks a tetrahedron. The room senses that a higher dimension has entered.* This was what happened when Swami Chidananda entered a room.

27 Oct. 2018

74. *Good relationships are a privilege won with sincerity.*
20 November 2014

75. *Yoga is the antidote for growing up.*

76. *The void says nothing and the wise person listens carefully.*
11 Aug. 2005

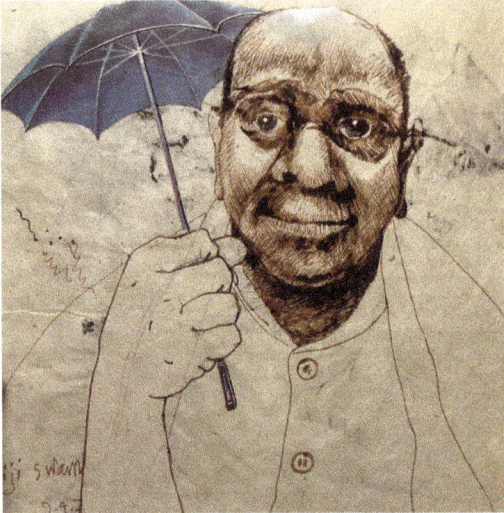

Fig. 8 "Having Fun" - Drawing of a swami at Sivananda Ashram 1971

77. *Ignorance always destroys itself, leaving truth in its absence.*

6 Oct. 2013

78. *Ego doesn't like silence.*   *2011*

79. *In the West, there is a statement in Latin that proclaims, "Credio ex nihilo" meaning "something comes from nothing".*
The Gita says, "Non-being (Asat) does not come into being; being cannot disappear." (Vedanta does not accept "Credio ex nihilo".)

80. *This world is a heart ache, it is the company of saints and sages that ease the pain.*

3 March 2014

81. *In Christianity, your will has to be replaced with God's will.*
In Hinduism, your will is an illusion.   *2018*

82. *Feelings produce thoughts that become deeds. Deeds produce effects, which are felt and in turn produce feelings. Round and round it goes.*

83. *For the Occidental "Nothingness" is the nature of death.*
    For the Oriental "No thingness" is the nature of death.

84. *Lots of people worry about Jesus coming....they need to worry more about their going!*

    1968

85. *Do your opinions liberate or confine you? That's the question.*

86. *Nothing ..... the nature of deep sleep*
    No thing ..... the nature of enlightenment

    1 Jan 1972

87. *A person gets up in the morning and asks, "What am I going to do today?" A seeker gets up and emphatically states "Today I need to know who I really am."*

    11 August 2016 - Sitting on the couch

88. *Misery is ignorance's celebration ....*

89. *The man of God renounces his desires quietly and to himself.*

90. *REALITY isn't an obstacle.*
Commentary: What is real is not to be dismissed as unwanted or to be thought of as an obstacle. Reality provides your best opportunity to become what you are before you forget who you are.

12 / 22 / 2013

91. *People think their mind does everything they want it to do.*
   In truth, people do everything their mind tells them to do.
   We are not our mind. The mind and we are related, the way a knot is to related to a loop of string.

20 Jan 1979

92. *If we can't get along with our neighbors on earth, how are we going to get along with our neighbors from space when they finally arrive?*

Sept. 22, 2017

93. *I suspect God simply can't understand what evil could be.*
   As the creator of everything, he certainly didn't create evil.
   Perhaps then, good and evil do not really exist. Maybe they are of a human origin.

27 Jul 1990 - Mt. Airy, MD

94.   *Remember to kiss the world goodbye when you leave.*
      It has been tough love at its best.

                                                            2017

95.   *Life is like a cloud, here one minute, there in another*
      and gone before you know It ….. People live as if it
      were as solid as a rock.

                                                    28 August 1971

96.   *Success for the ego is failure for the soul.*

97.   *The curse of feeling special …*
              the burden of feeling unique …
                      denies the Self its spirit.

                              1970's - Revised thought of, July 30, 2020

98.   *A tree is just a tree.*
      A rock is just a rock.
      Nothing is bound until claimed by the mind.

99.   *Spiritual dangers are rarely boldly announced.*
      They usually present themselves as sweet and pleasing.

                                      Dallastown, PA – 19 Jan 1977

100. *Grace is denied a foothold, when "something came from nothing" is believed.*

Sunday, 16 June 2013

101. *Speaking about consciousness is like using a shadow to look for light.*

17 Aug 1992

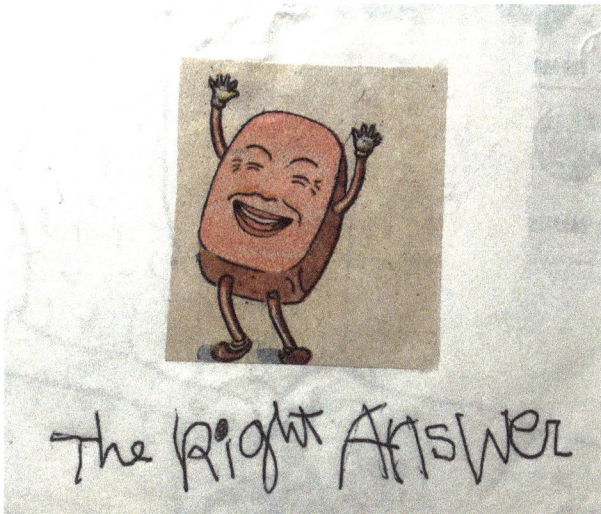

Fig. 9 The Right Answer

102. *"I don't go to church much; I go to Jesus, Durga, Rama, Siva, Mary, Meenakshi and all the rest of cosmic pantheon."*

A comet after having a conversation with a churchitarian —5/8/2015

103. *The more agitated the mind, the longer the evolution.*

1970 Rishikesh, India

104. *Do you answer all the questions, or question all the answers?*

If the former, you are a student. If the latter, you are seeker.

10 May 1989

105. *Life is simple.....be good, do good and you're basically done.*

30 Aug. 2017

106. *Bliss is the effect of wholeness.*

India 1970

107. *When you get around to calling on God, don't wait till it has to be a 911 call.*

26 Nov 1990

108. *Fear not, nothing will never happen.*

109. *Discipline is nothing in comparison to self-discipline.*

110. *If it can fail, it will fail. If it can't fail it doesn't exist.*

2010

111. *Remember authors, your pencil has an eraser.*

13 Sept. 2020

Chapter 3
Heavy Light

Fig. 10 Himalayas- 1971

Pundit at a night discourse on the Upanishads by the Ganges at Laksman
Jhula Ashram

112. *Scholars have all the questions. Sages have the answers.*

113. *More powerful than the pen is the person that holds it.*

18 Jan 1989

114. *Two wrongs make an evil.*

9-2-2002

115. *Without love … life is dangerous.*

2018

116. *Three letters that may terrify: IRS, FBI, CIA, KGB, KKK, and GOD*

1979

117. *Shadows don't have shadows.*   **30 Aug. 2017**

118. *The sum total of the universe is zero.*

Field Structure physics 101 Ancient comet

119. *The problem with heaven is that you have to die to get there.*

Mt. Airy - 12-8-98

120. *How many of us are like rugs?*
    We lie around all day, day after day,
        in the end we are completely worn out.

Mar. 18, 2014

121. *The Void's advice is .... "Avoid nothing!"*

9/23/2005 8PM

122. *There are no black holes ... only black paint.*

123. *Fear of fear is not the point.*
    The deep and penetrating fear is in the realization that there may not be a point.

Admittedly highly controversial - Monday, 31 December 2012
Modified 12 Oct 2020

124. *There are many religions.*
    Which one is the true one?
    On this they all agree.
    *Ask any of them and they'll all tell you the same thing .... "**mine**"!*
Dec 1976

Fig. 11 It's Heavy

125. *You can't liberate others until you can liberate yourself.*

Dec. 13, 2018

126. *"How about all the TIME we have killed?*
Will SPACE have its revenge?"

Jan 2006

127. *Look for the future in the present.*

Nov. 1976

128. *America – Integrate or disintegrate !*

129. *In the forest wild ... where a visit I just made ... I*
found this creature sitting motionless on a log and
to my surprise, it was me.

Revised thought of 1970's > July 30, 2020

130. *Nothing never becomes something, and something*
never becomes nothing.
I know full well Quantum Mechanics and General
Relativity implicitly refute this statements.

8th April 2017 @ 1:23 AM

131. *It's all about exchanging the lower case self for the*
upper case Self; the local for the non-local Totality.

2018

132. *Physics studies waves (plural). Metaphysics studies ocean (singular).*

2018

133. *Yer command of language can keep you ignamunt. Actions confirm or disprove it.* *28/10/2020*

134. *We will achieve immortality with a body when we have no more karmic obligation, but when we no longer have any karmic obligation, we no longer would find a body useful. It would be a limitation we would like to discard so that we can live in spirit alone, a far more useful form of existence. If you can imagine life without a body and an ego, you will know what the experience of death will be like.*

12-4-2017 @ 9.17PM

135. *How we think, affects the world. The world is the effect of our thinking.*

28 Dec. 2018

136. *Go ahead criticize America .....it might be useful to tamp down the hubris least we grow arrogant.*

June 14, 201

137. *The metaphysics of a knot is the string.*

2015

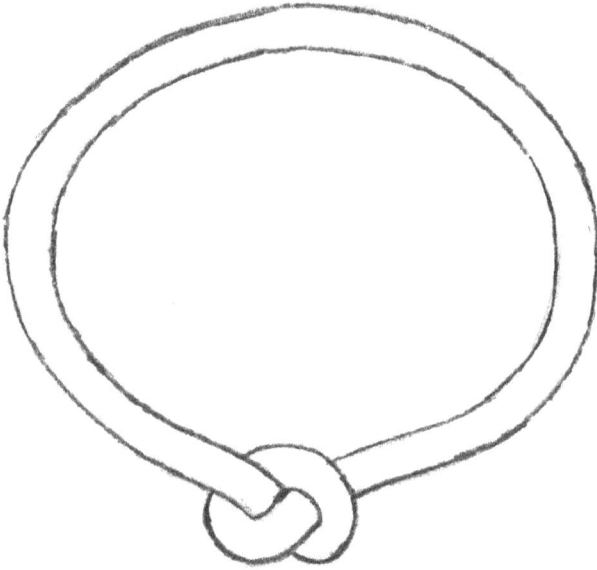

Fig. 12 Knot on a string loop

138. *After enlightenment, the knot doesn't worship the string.*
Why? Because the knot realizes it is string ....

8 May 1982

139. *Be advised, your sphere of awareness may actually be a circle of containment.*

6 Jun 1972

140. *The cultured mind is like a pair of old shoes; easy to get into and out of again.*

9 Nov 1984

141. *Your Deity is with you as you.*

2019

142. *Behind it all is everything.*

10 Apr 1988

143. *A religion that doesn't sing ... is a religion in mourning.*

9-11-15

144. *What amazes me is how there are raving ego maniacs pretending to be spiritual people who can keep their bullshit smelling like a rose for years on end so their followers will be eager to pay for a sniff.*

- 28 August 2017

145. *Hinduism solves the problem of finding the meaning of life by offering an explanation that voids the need to ask for an explanation.*

2018

146. *You get to a point in life where you see the edge and say, "Finally!"*

Oct. -2014

147. *The problem with Hinduism is that so much was explained to me I can't possibly remember it all.*

2018

Chapter 4
Pathing Observations

"Genius is more often found in a cracked pot than in a whole one."

E. B White, American

Fig. 13 Hallen Street – South African asking me to throw the I Ching for him at the Sivananda Ashram, Rishikesh, India – 1971

148. *What's important is not so much in having patience, but in being able not to lose it.*

October 3rd 2009

149. *It's a big asset to know how to do something, but of more value is having the determination to try and do something when you don't really know how it's done.*

150. *Getting old is interesting ... Everything you took for granted now demands your attention.*

2019

151. *Usually I am more impressed with the question than I am with the answer.*

11-08-2006 - dawn on a rainy day

152. *The only way to solve a problem is to admit there is one.*

153. *You are what you know. You cannot know anything without becoming it in some way.*

154. *Don't reject what you don't know until you under-stand it.*

19 August 2020

155. *If you can't love your neighbor, and you can't even like your neighbor, at least tolerate your neighbor.*

2 July 2018

156. *Sending a new theory to a science journal is like sending a love letter to a robot.*   July 28, 2019

157. *To the ignorant, truth seems impossible.*
To the truthful, ignorance is intolerable.
Truth doesn't hurt, facing your ignorance hurts.

While carving a swan - Shop 2-11-2011

158. *Scholars have all the questions. Sages the answers.*

159. *Most folks know life by the bridge they take over it.*

Nepal 1970

160. *Looking around at what passes for normal; who would want to be normal?*

17 Nov. 2012   7:43 PM

161. *Follow your dream ..... without falling asleep.*

18 Jan 1985

162. *Half of my problems are the whole of my problems.*

3 Oct. 2016

163. *Overcoming imperfections is the way to perfection.*

28 Jun 1986

164. *Big Ideas are often small when compared to the effort it takes to execute them .... Good Luck!*

Sept. 27, 2012

165. *The Divine serves all. Religions serve a chosen few.*

166. Reality keeps us from falling asleep while dreaming of what could be.

16 June 2013

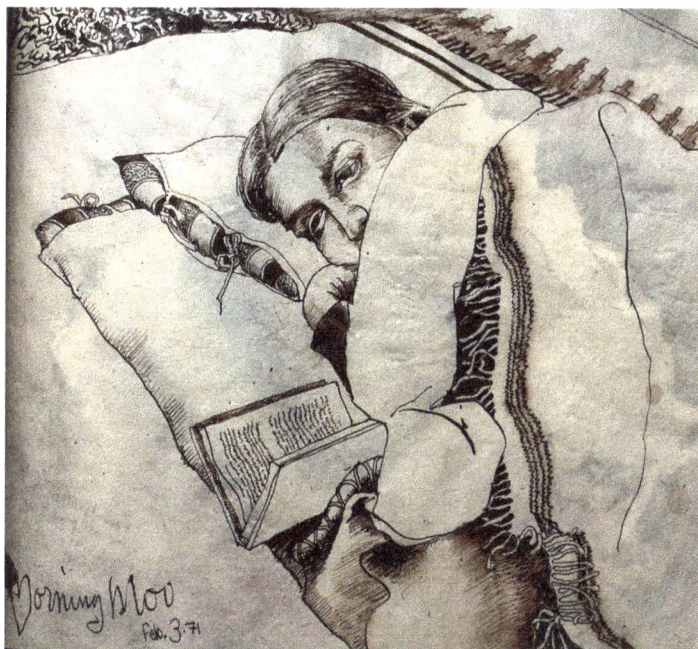

Fig. 14 Early morning - Moo in her bedroll at the Ashram 1971

167. *What good is a physics that doesn't mean anything and inversely, what good is a metaphysics that has no physical significance?*

168. *A locality has no meaning[1] without a Totality for a context, and inversely a Totality that cannot produce a locality is worthless.*

Mt. Airy 2016

---

1   For example, Big Bang is a physics that ends in the extinction of all life in the universe. If that is what the universe is all about, we live in a meaningless universe.

169. *The universe is the one song from which all songs are derived.*

7:30 AM on 1/30/2015

170. *The difference between a believer and a knower is that a believer talks a lot and a knower has no compulsion to speak.*

8 Feb 1993

171. *The difference between earth and hell is that on earth, at least, there are a few saints and sages among us.*

Dec 1984

172. *The first step is as important as the last step.*

27 April 2017

173. *Out of nothing, comes nothing.*

30 Aug. 2017

174. *You don't live in a body. The body lives in you.*

4th Oct. 2015

175. *It's more important to do what you have to do …
than do what you want to do. But when one is operating from one's true center, what one has to do is also what one wants to do.*

176. *It's fine not to do something you can't justify.
It is NOT fine to justify what you can't do.*

1 Jan. 1984

177. *It is of no help to be moving when you're trying to cover the entire universe.*

Pausing on a rock pile in the Mohave Desert 1973

Fig. 15 The Seeker   1971

178. *There are two kinds of intelligence.*
The kind that accumulated through experience and the kind that occurs as spontaneous intuition. The former comes from relative experience and the latter from the Absolute.

179. *Reality is an endless story told in increments of time.*

6 September 2014

180. *I'm not a hell and damnation Christian. I love God and Goddess. I don't fear them. Besides, God and Goddess are my parents!*

19 December 2013

181. *In Christianity you have two opportunities, hope and pray.*
In Yoga-Vedanta, the opportunities are mediate and realize.

2014

182. *In every situation there is its locality and its Totality. Dealing with the locality will have a temporary effect.*
Dealing with the Totality will have a lasting effect.

2-3-2015

27 Oct. 2018

183. *I may have a pretty good idea about how the universe works, but I will never understand why my mattress keeps sliding off the bed.*

Apr. -20 2009

Fig. 16 Problems with my bed   1968

184. *The way to avoid a humiliation is to learn humility.*

185. *Heaven doesn't accept excuses.*

2018

186. *Hinduism solved the problem of describing the meaning of life by offering an explanation that eliminates the need for an explanation!*

July 28, 2019

187. *My body and mind, and all that goes with them, is confining. It is in my soul where freedom is to be found.*

2018

188. *There is more to it than happy.*

30 Aug. 2017

189. *If I had to choose between the past and the future, I'd abstain.*

23 Jan 2017

190. *While great forces in the hands of small minds are tearing the world apart, great minds are quietly constructing the new world to come.*

22 November 2013

191. *Great people are known more for what they gave away then what they kept.*

25 Jun 1985

192. *The Problem with Christianity as explained to me was that too little was explained to me.*

2018

193. *Want to go to hell? It's easy! Just keep on thinking hellish thoughts and doing hellish deeds.*

March 2019

194. *The nice thing about enlightenment is that you don't have to run all over the place looking for it.*

Sunbeam, new moon, July 16, 2015

195. *A sure sign you are getting old if instead of taking steps, you shuffle along.*

196. *Scientists expect something, or they don't bother. Sages expect nothing and so obtain their every wish, made easier by having few if any wishes.*

Durban, RSA - Oct 1971, revised 12 Oct. 2020

197. *Religion is a belief system. Without belief, it is nothing.*
Yoga is a knowledge system. Without knowing, it is just smoke and mirrors.

28 August 1971

198. *The best way to visualize yourself in the cosmos is to visualize the cosmos in yourself.*

199. *God doesn't scare me … but some humans do.*

Sept. 8ᵗʰ, 2020

Fig. 17 Swami Chidananda meditating   1971

200. *Why is it that those that come the farthest, get there first?*

2 –Dec -2014

201. *A delusion of grandeur is in being proud that your life boat came off the S. S. Titanic.*

In the workshop   24 August 2013

202. *There are two kinds of boys. One is born with a screwdriver. The other is born with a hammer. The former screw things up and the latter nail things down.*

1970

203. *It's a mistake to possess anything, and it's a crime not to use what you're given.*

29 Sep. 1985

204. *In carpentry, as in life, it is easier to make an outside surface square and an inside surface round.*

Cuenca, Ecuador - May 1972

205. *Accumulate virtues. They are your protection in a world of vicissitudes.*

206. **Cartoon Character –** *Terry Bull*

207. *Cause >> of interest to Orientals*
    Effect >> of interest to Occidentals

Nov. 2019

208. *The problem with Hinduism is that there are a mind-numbing amount of things to remember and then be told reality is beyond description!*

July 28, 2019

209. *Conservation of Energy is a fundamental property of physics.*
    Conservation of Being is a fundamental property of metaphysics.

2016

210. *If having to remember everything about Hinduism that was explained to me is a requirement to gain enlightenment, I'll never make it.*

2020

211. *Listen to what is being said, not who is saying it.*

Election eve, November 6th, 2012

Chapter 5
Random Callings

Fig. 18 Swami Krishnananda and a visiting yogi giving a satsang at
the Sivananda Ashram - 1971

212. *When the time comes, it's here.*

at the shop   7/8/2011

213. *What do you put on a pig's rash?*
.... *Oinkment !*

16 July 2015

214. *Woke up, looked in the mirror, and exclaimed, "yikes!"*

24 August 2013
In the workshop

215. *The Salivation Army is a pack of hungry dogs.*

10 Jan 1989

216. *The earth is a vehicle waiting for a driver.*

July 30, 2020

217. *Se!!*

18 Sept 2018

218. **Sign on a driveway gate***: "There is nothing of value on this property, including you."*

1982

219. *There is only one revolution, the change from igno-rance to truth.*
It has nothing to do with politics, but politics should have everything to do with it.

Cuenca, Ecuador 26 Apr 1972

220. *The noun "The Overlook" and the verb "To Overlook" are opposite experiences.*

221. *If the question "who am I?" doesn't have any mean-ing, what the hell is the matter with you?*

7ᵗʰ Oct. 2015 / Aug. 19, Aug. 2020

222. *People who present you with problems are really people asking for solutions.*

17 Sep 1987

223. *In begging with a hole in your hat, you'll never get a head or even a tail.*

July 30, 2020

224. *Physics is the awareness of field objects. Metaphysics is the awareness that everything is a field of force.*

5 December 2011

225. *Opinion is the product of a perception. Knowledge is the product of experience.*

    23 Jun 1993 revised 12 Sep 1993 then again 16 Mar 2014

226. *In response to fear ... horrible things are done.*

    16 Nov 2017

227. *Look with your eyes .... See with your heart.*

    24 August 1976

228. *Life is passing ... introduce yourself.*

229. *If you count to three, you missed the moment.*

    March 2013

230. *Food is a growing problem.*

231. *Consciousness organizes the universe instantly and does this all the time!*   pr.15-2014

232. *If there is a day, there's a way....*

    24-March 1995

233. *How the world works is philosophy. How to work with the world is engineering.*

1985

234. *However you want me is how you should leave me.*

16 Dec 1989

235. *Black Holes are actually reality's No-Fly zones.*

July 31, 2018

236. *Arty Fishel is a playboy and his younger brother Benny Fishel is always trying to make up for his brother's shortcomings.*

1982

237. *Clouds reveal the turbulence.*

Jan. 25, 2014

238. *In a pile of stuff, why is the last one always the one being looked for ?*

Fig. 19 Her Duck   1968

239. *When the cosmos comes a-calling. I hope your number is in the book.*

28 Jun 1989

240. *The shortest distance between one day and the next is through the shadow that separates them.*

At 38,000 feet on route to India Feb 1977

241. *My psychic evaluation report is finally in .... Those who are sure I'm nuts can now explain it to me.*

November 30, 2012

242. *If you are going to think .... Think big.*

1980

Chapter 6
Leaves Arrive

Fig. 20 Moo by the Ganges in spate - Rishikesh, Himalayas - 1971

243. *Don't see a wall …. see a door !*
These words of wisdom came out of the mouth of Giovanna Brandi when she was three years old in 1973.

244. *The whatchamacallits and the whosits are never clear about their intentions.*
3-18-2014

245. *It's not where you are … it's what you are that is meaningful.*
Feb. 5th, 2016

246. *The most important step in a journey is the first one.*
25 April 2017

247. *There's truth in fiction and that's a fact.*
May, 19, 2010

248. *The reward for simplicity is peace.*
Sept. 28, 2017

249. *There are a hundred million billion stars in the sky. One of them obliterates all the rest.*
Mt. Airy, MD 1 Jan 1990

250. *Childhood was back when Time was a toy !*

4/18/2013   1 AM

251. *Which is more important ... to have wings or to know how to fly?*

23 Dec 1988

252. *Humans use their spirits, for the same reason birds use their wings.*

253. *Staying in one place ... makes a rock happy. Nothing annoys a rock more than being moved. Landslides are infuriating!*

254. *Rocks love a blanket of snow on a cold winter's night.*

This is my favorite passing comet   Nov. 20, 2017

255. *Knowing right you have to know wrong.*

July 14, 2017

256. *Take time to paradigm.*

June 29, 2019

257. *Wherever you are ……….. there you are !*

Fig. 21 A Vision   1971

258. *The push-pull aspects of your life make rhythms.*
The circular turnings account for its melody.

259. *Knowledge is two-dimensional .... Experience is three.*

260. *If I had a moment to spare. I would tell you everything in an instant.*

23 Nov. 2012 and then again 10 Nov. 2014

261. *Your guess is as good as mind.*

5 November 2014

Fig. 22 Our Yoga/Vedanta teacher Swami Tejomayananda at the Sivananda Ashram

1971

262. *Half-baked knowledge looks for an oven.*

2018

263. *Why is creativity so compelling? Because in the creative moment, there can be hours of fascination.*

10/19/2012 11:51pm

264. *Mediation inspires wisdom......what are you waiting for?*

2015

265. *There they were, minutes lying on the ground dead and dying. Somebody had time to kill.*

2013

266. **Cartoon Character.** - *Sue Mac*

Fig. 23 A Blown Mind Interlude in Ecuador   1969

267. *The point of your point is pointless.*

Oct. 8 -2015

268. *At night, flowers close. In the day, they open ...*
There is beauty in that !

24 June 2015

269. *Measure friends by what they say when you're not*
around them.

13 Nov 1983

270. *I look at our forest of Amaryllis in full bloom and wonder, if I, in their eyes, am as beautiful as they are in mine?*
I got the feeling I'm not even close.

Friday, April 26, 2019

271. *At the center of everything is stillness…*

Oct. 10 -2014

272. *"To know a book by how it feels is how a blind person reads.*

1 Aug. 2020

273. *The sun can't see darkness … neither can the saint or sage see sin.*

Aug. 1975

274. *The differences between "nowhere" and "now here" is space.*

275. *In a building full of doors, we can be sure about which door leads out. It is the one we used to come in.*

Jan. 18 – 2014 5:25 AM

Chapter 7
Ar Tick U La tions

Fig. 24 Rug & Socks   South Africa - 1972

276. *If you were ice cream cone, I'd give you a licking.*
2018

277. *We can't be everything, but aspiring to be nothing isn't very inspirational.*

1973

278. *Body and mind are confining. It is with my soul that freedom is to be found.*

2018

279. *We are not individuals, we are undividables.*

1 Jan 1972

280. *Two thieving birds on a limb watching a lady load a bird feeder: one bird says to the other, "I wonder why she's doing that. Doesn't she realize we are going to steal it the moment she walks away?"*

2015

281. *It's not where you are … it's what you are that is meaningful.*

Feb. 5th, 2016,

282. *I don't like to use an alarm clock to time my meditation. It disturbs my sleep.*

May 17th. 2016

283. *Motion – Emotion ... are the same thing.*

> July 30, 2020

284. *Reality keeps us from falling asleep while dreaming of what could be.*

> 16 June 2013

285. *You know you are a rednecker if you use a bumper sticker to cover body rust.*

286. *The head turned tails and threw through away his chances.*

> August 21, 2020

287. *The severe fever never ever severed the clever lever endeavour.*

> July 30, 2020 revised 15 Aug. 2020 revised again 28 Aug 2020

288. *Having nothing to say does not require you to speak.*

> Aug. 30, 2017

Fig. 25 The old swami at the evening satsang in the Bhajan Hall - 1970

289. *I may not know who YOU is, but I know who you are.*

Apr. 23, 2011 - 1:30 AM

290. *There are two ways to find out if your boat leaks.*
Put it in the water, or take it out.

23 Dec

291. *If you see the forest, but not the trees, you're a visionary. If you see the trees, but not the forest, you're a realist.*

2018

292. *Always know how to get out of a situation before you get in.*

4 June 2015 - Homeless

293. *Evil is wilful ignorance.*

Someone said - 31 December 2012

294. **A well prepared cartoon character –** *Justin Case*

2019

295. *Don't just chew on the truth; it's best when swallowed whole.*

13 Sep 1995

296. *Loving your country does not mean you have to love its weaknesses.*

4 Feb, 2017

297. *Experience the equation ... to truly understand its meaning.*

2020

298. *In cosmology, if the equation doesn't equal zero, it's wrong.*

2020

299. *Speculation is usually inconsequential, but without it break-throughs are impossible.* *2020*

300. *Name for a tavern ..... "What Ales You"*

301. *Life isn't a category....It's an allegory.* January, 2008

302. *Don't be a heel ... Tip Toe To Totality.*

Chapter 8
Money Honey

Fig. 26 Found in the Bethesda Naval Hospital chapel while a patient looking for a quiet room to meditate – 1967

303. *To feed my cow, I sell her milk ...... that makes us both happy.*

Aug. 1st, 2020

304. *There are two kinds of people. Those who want to make a living and those who want to make a killing.*
16 Nov 2017

305. *Tax collectors are like mosquitoes. It's hard to see their usefulness when you're being bitten.*

305. *The sad truth is the only way many folks have of knowing whether they are doing right, or not, is whether or not they are getting paid.*
15 Jul 1972

306. *Money, sex and fame ... won't nourish the soul and may tarnish it.*
new moon – 20 November 2014

307. *Heard in a community kitchen queue, "I wouldn't work if you paid me."*

308. In the workshop I wrote on the wall, *"These prices reflect my interest in making a living, rather than my attempt to make a killing,* and thought that was ever so virtuous. A few years later an employee scribbled under the statement: *This should read, "These prices reflect my interest in making a killing so I can afford to pay my employees a decent living!"*

Dallastown, PA   1978

309. *Banks give money to those who have it. Government gives money to those who don't.* This is how capitalism and socialism can work together for the good of all.

In the workshop – Spring 2018

310. *Make a lot of sense, before making a lot of dollars.*

2016

311. *When it's offered, wisdom is often regarded as worthless.*
When it's needed, it can't be bought for love nor money.

Chapter 9
Seen Together

Fig. 27 1969 Drawing of a dream had in Ecuador about my wife and
I having to face three huge waves, each succeeding the former in size.
And they did indeed break over us and yet we survived.

312. *I had to explain to our host in India that our mar-*
riage was not arranged by our parents. God made
all the arrangements.   July 28, 2019

313. *To know divine love, know human love.*

10 Dec. 2011

early in a 14 hour meditation marathon

314. *He asked: "Darling, when do you know you are enlightened?"*
She answered: "When you know every moment of your life that you and the universe are inseparable!"

May 22, 2012

315. *When it happens for love, it happens best.*

316. *How could we have known that all the messing around we did in our twenties would lead to us baby-sitting the grandkids on New Year's Eve?*

Dec. 31st, 2016

317. *Only a Siva knows how to love a Parvati.*

While looking at a sunset 21 Dec -2014

318. *Time is masculine. Space is feminine.*

319. *Only a lover can withstand eternity.*

Don Briddell

320. **Question:** *What sermon is appropriate for a wedding night?*
Answer: The Sermon on the Mount.

1-27-2005

321. *If you come in my house and catch my wife with her lover, that's alright, we're often seen together!*

30 Jan 1989

322. *Fortunately, humor replaces sex in one's old age. The good thing about humor is that it can be had anywhere, anytime and with anyone.*

2017

323. *Old fires can't burn again. This applies to old flames.*

Dec. 2012

324. *Successful marriages are not determined by how thrilling they were, but by now well the difficulties were endured.* 8 Aug 1976

Fig. 28 Journal entry - India   1971

325. *You can't make love. You can only celebrate its discovery!*

326. *You know you're getting older when every conversation begins with,*
"What did ya say?"

327. *House dust at twenty-five went unnoticed. At seventy-five it's everywhere!*

2019

328. *When God decided to split-up humans into male and female, it proved he had a sense of humor.*

Dec. 6, 2018

329. *One way to put out an argument ... is to smother it with kisses.*

May 12, 2019

330. *Do this. Do that. And while you are at it, do the other thing.*

Such is married life .. 9 Nov 1984

331. *A baby is not fully human until its first laugh.*

3/31/2014

332. *I've learned over the years the good times are what goes on between your ears, not between your legs.*

333. *If I told you what it takes to be a man, women would be annoyed and men would be dumfounded.*

July 7, 2017

Chapter 10
The Facts of Life

Fig. 29 Swami giving an evening discourse on the Ramayana at the
Sivananda Ashram - 1971

334. *The loudest voices are usually the ones with the least to say, except for the one yelling, FIRE!*

2020

335. *For thinkers, the path of truth is path-o-logical.*

336. *I've come to the conclusion that the only way to keep my workshop clean is to never use it.*

16 July 2018

337. *With age, we begin to value wisdom over cleverness.*

2015

338. *Watching TV is the mind being nursed by the media.*

21 April 1992

396. *There are a million ways to get into trouble, and only one way to avoid it.*

7 April 1992

340. *Youth see life without an ending. Elders see eternal life.*

26 May 1990 then rethought 20 November 2014

341. *We are all born with truths called "Talents".*

342. *The Big Bang says it all started from nothing and the whole thing will end up fading into nothing. The theory of General Relativity concludes the universe is programmed to annihilate itself...... "Have a nice day!"*

Oct. 2nd, 2007

343. *Truth relieves pain.*
Ignorance causes pain.

August 19, 2020

344. *You do not become strong by protecting your muscles from work.*
Likewise, to have full use of your spirit put it to constant use.

8 Mar 1976

345. *You don't need to pave the world with leather. All you need is a pair of shoes.* This is a paraphrase of an old Indian proverb which I heard from Swami Chidananda.

346. *The Internet gives the bad guys the same opportunity as it does the good guys. Life lets you choose!*

14 Aug. 2015

347. *In some ways a knife is like the ego. It can cut through everything but itself.*

3 Feb 1973

348. *The earth can miss the rain, but the rain can never miss the earth.*
Such is the relationship between God and mankind.

Dallastown, PA – 1 Nov 1977

349. *If there is one idea in a world of possible ideas that does not belong in the natural world, it is the idea of there being a singularity.*

Feb. 18, 2014 - 5:05AM

350. *Open up by shutting up.*

20 Aug. 2011 11:57 PM

351. *My body and mind are confining. It is my soul wherein freedom can be found.*

2018

352. *If truth makes you angry, ignorance hides in the heart.*

353. *I got lost looking for myself …. I think one has to!*
1990

354. *Mankind needs society like a horse needs a rider.*

355. *Missing the point is a good thing if you are a sword swallower.*

356. *When they told me I was grown up I felt like I'd done something foolish.*
22 May 1975

357. *Those headlights you see that have you frozen in your tracks is approaching reality.*
Dawn   20 Jan 2013

358. *The world of nature includes the world of humankind, but seldom in the affairs of government and industry is nature considered, much less included.*
Jan 1979

359. *If you can't explain everything, then you can't explain anything. That is why sages speak little and maintain silence.*

19 June 2013

360. *Ignorance is personal .... Truth is impersonal.*

30 Aug. 2017

361. *Nothing you can give can ever be taken from you.*

362. *Forget what you hate. Remember what you love.*

22 Feb 2010

363. *The problem with most bucket lists is that by the time you want to use the bucket, it's rusted through.*

Mar. 18, 2018 when carving a pintail.

364. *The vehicle used by freedom is truth.*

Dallastown, PA. - 2 Nov. 1979

365. *Facts are beliefs no one has as yet successfully challenged.*

18 Sept 2018

366. *Unfortunately, facts can't speak for themselves. They rely on the human voice.*

14 May 2018 - at bedtime

367. *Human beings are savages. A venomous snake does not have a sense of right and wrong. Human beings have that sense and violate its injunctions with impunity !*

July 28, 2019

368. *Youth want to know the purpose. Elders want to know the principle.*

26 August 1990

369. *Each and every life is the shortest possible cut there is to understanding.*

370. *Without enlightenment ... there is only doubt.*

July 30, 2020

371. *The arrogance of ignorance says, because I don't know, you don't know either.*

Dec. 4, 2017

372. *You can take as many breaths as you want, but try not to take your last one.*

2017

373. *Sure, I've got a dream, but I want reality.*

374. *Forget the deep water, you can drown in the shallows.*

25 Jan-2015

375.

As

you

get older,

the notes

you post

to yourself

get

bigger

376. *What we want, is to talk without being told what to say.*

Sunday,   26 February 2012

377. *Being is a potential ....*
Becoming is a force.

Rehoboth Beach, DE – 17 September 2013

378. *You can't reject what you are, only what you are not.*

29 September 1985

379. *It may not be bad to be poor, but it certainly isn't good.*

Botha's Hill, South Africa   14 Jul 1986

Chapter 11
Poetree

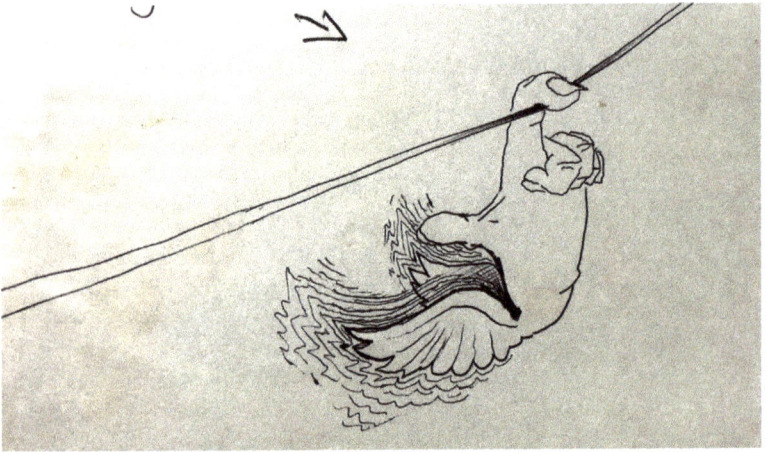

Fig. 30   Ecuador - 1969

380. *The written word is for those who forget.*

12 Mar 1972

381. *The sun behind the clouds...*
     The clouds above the rain...
          The rain pounds the umbrella...
               Below my feet are wet.

382. *Out of nowhere a dog barks .... who jumps?*

Rishikesh, India   1971

383. *Too often people are in religion not to develop spiritually, but to fortify themselves psychologically.*

384. *Pay attention to the poets .... You need them, and they know what you need.*

31 Jan 1985

385. Haiku:
     Waiting for pizza
     In a crowded restaurant
     Toppings cost a lot

386. *I love wrens. I love my cat. Cat kills wrens. Wrens agitate cats. I still love wrens and cats.*

16 Sept. 2015 - Dumfounded

387. Haiku:

> *Water knows no wait*
> *My soul in eternity*
> *Thank God for the laugh*

19 Jun 1985

388. Haiku

> *Brush raised in awe*
> *The artist waits the moment*
> *The paint wants to dry*

7 Jun 1985

389. *A blank ceiling high from the floor, ah, a place of peace in a crowded room.*

24 Aug 1975

390. *You and I are one. Add to, take from, still one. All we need to know......Done!*

Aug. 1st, 2020

391. *With you, as you, aren't we ?*

1985

392. *Seems to me, there's a beautiful moon out tonight.*
Seems to me there's a comet in sight.
It's going to be a beautiful day,
because it's been a glorious night.

Aug. 1ˢᵗ, 2020

393. *If you are wondering why birds fly, birds ARE the sky.*

Aug. 1ˢᵗ, 2020

394. *Camels and kids run with the train as it starts over the white baked plains ... who remembers names?*

on a train crossing north India 1970

Fig. 31 Ann Berliner   1971

91

Chapter 12
On Art

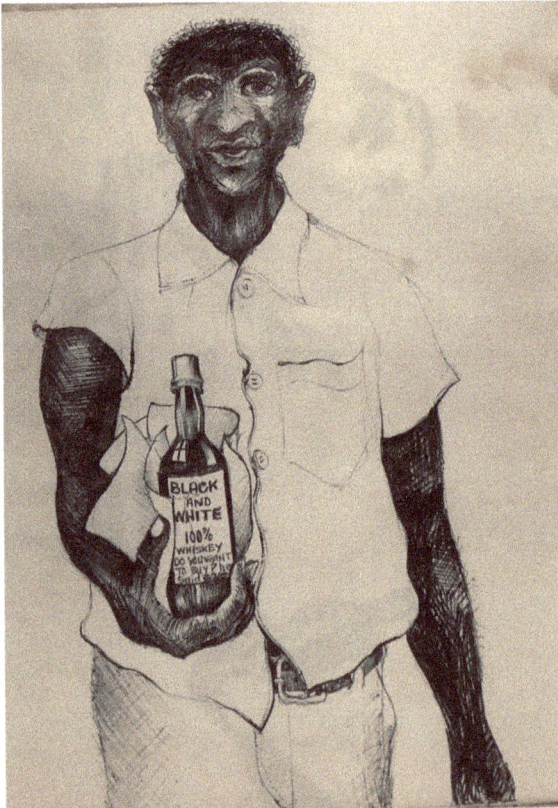

Fig. 32 Tempting us with bootleg Black and White Whiskey, we decline as Moo and I dined at the Hotel Turismo, Esmeraldas, Ecuador.

1969

395. *For artists, having a patron is like a bird finding a birdfeeder.*

March 20

396. *Difficulty in execution does not make a work of art better.*
It is the sense of completeness surrounding the work that gives it vitality.

28 Jul 1976

397. *Carving is like life …*
It is not what you take away for which you are remembered.
It is for what you leave behind that you will be judged.

17 Mar 1981

398. *The wood sculptor explained, "My knives have seen the glory."*

Sunday, 26 February 2012

399. *For artists, the income maybe meagre, but the out-come may be glorious!* Dawn 20 Jan 2013

400. *The nice thing about art is that while to be honest no one really needs it, yet when civilizations are remembered, it is their art that reveals their glory.*

12 Oct 1987

401. *Art for the artist is agony. It is to see what the agony can become that is so compelling.*

5 March 1982

402. *When an artist has a calling, give him or her time to explain what they heard in the medium of their choosing.*

16 Jan 1987

403. *Everything is important in its proper place. The artist finds the place.*

Malaysia 1970

404. *There are times when art and math get along …. such as in number painting.*

November 27, 2013

405. *Laborers worry over how much they've done. Craftspeople worry over what they are doing. Artists worry over the outcome.* 16 Mar 2014

Fig. 33 Giving up on us, he goes over a few tables and finds a purchaser.

1968

406. *Technique is the artist's way of saying less to say it better.*

First attempt 1976

Revised 3-17-2014

407. *It's the artists and poets that help you to become what you know and know what you have become.*

29 September 1985

Fig. 34 On leaving, we observe how it all ended   1969

408. *Art is the tried and true way humanity has been able to escape the limitations of time and space.*

21 August 2020

409. *The problem with art schools is that they don't teach the business of art. It is like giving the student a brush and canvas, but not supplying the paint.*

2020

410. *If you realize your connection to Totality, you can paint a miracle.*

India 1971

411. *Trying to understand art is like trying to understand the song of a bird? You may not understand it but yet thoroughly enjoy it.*

It is to be enjoyed without the compulsion to know what it means.

412. *To make an art form out of work is to transcend it.*

Kuala Lumpur, Malaysia Aug 1970

413. *When people's feelings are tender, there is no room for greatness.*

414. *In repeating a lie often enough, it is taken to be a truth.*

2020

415. *The universe talks to those who ask questions.*

2020

416. *Maybe ignorance is the failure to see what God intended.*

Fig. 35 Baba Ramdas drawn from life at New Delhi, India 1971

Holding the question
while
awaiting another
comet to pass....
this is a stopping place,
but not the end of it.

Mt. Airy, Maryland
USA